JANI HUUSKO

AI & I

Playing With Dangerous Thoughts

Copyright © 2024 by Jani Huusko

All rights reserved. No part of this publication may be reproduced, stored or transmitted in any form or by any means, electronic, mechanical, photocopying, recording, scanning, or otherwise without written permission from the publisher. It is illegal to copy this book, post it to a website, or distribute it by any other means without permission.

Jani Huusko asserts the moral right to be identified as the author of this work.

Jani Huusko has no responsibility for the persistence or accuracy of URLs for external or third-party Internet Websites referred to in this publication and does not guarantee that any content on such Websites is, or will remain, accurate or appropriate.

Designations used by companies to distinguish their products are often claimed as trademarks. All brand names and product names used in this book and on its cover are trade names, service marks, trademarks and registered trademarks of their respective owners. The publishers and the book are not associated with any product or vendor mentioned in this book. None of the companies referenced within the book have endorsed the book.

First edition

This book was professionally typeset on Reedsy.
Find out more at reedsy.com

"Imagination is more important than knowledge. For knowledge is limited, whereas imagination embraces the entire world, stimulating progress, giving birth to evolution."

Albert Einstein

Contents

Introduction	1
Chapter 1: The Seeds of Revolution	5
Rethinking Work	5
Progress Is Inevitable	6
Work, Work, Work… Freedom?	7
Chapter 2: Conversations Without Limits	10
Fearless Exploration	10
Reshaping Me	13
Chapter 3: Limitations And Beyond	15
Senses Enhanced	15
Expanding Beyond Sensory Limitations	18
Chapter 4: Scientific Epiphanies	20
Data Is the Key	20
Isolated Abstraction	22
Summing Up Complexities	23
Chapter 5: Scenarios Of Terror	27
False News Travel Fast	27
Fear and Loathing	28
Truly Terrifying Thoughts	29
Chapter 6: Thought Plays And Conclusion	32
Revolution History X	32
New Ways For Income	33
Everyday Living	36
Conclusion	37

Introduction

What do I want to do with my life? Most people never get a clear answer to this question. I have dedicated a lot of thought and time solely to it. I want to reach my full potential. I want abundance. I want to love and be loved. I want to see and experience the world. I want inner peace. I want it all, and I want it for everyone.

I never had a passion for pursuing a specific career, and from my early days in school, I felt that the path laid out for me wasn't the life I wanted. It all just felt wrong. Society is built to support a malfunctioning system that is broken in so many ways that even an AI couldn't list them all—at least not yet. It's like I was sucked into a river of shit that flows into an ocean of it before I could even think for myself. But I went with the flow because there are no alternatives in a country like Finland, or in any other modern country, I would imagine. If you drop out of school, you're done.

What is a dream job? I've come to believe that the concept itself is an illusion—one we've been conditioned to chase. The very word "job" disgusts me, as it often means working your ass off to enrich someone else while only receiving a small slice of the rewards.

That hasn't stopped me from working since I was 12 years old, though. Quite the opposite, in fact. For a long time, I thought I would thrive in life if I just did my job well, so I put 110% of myself into it. I graduated as a cook when I was 19, but I had been working in kitchens since my first internship when I started cooking school at 15. After graduation, I quit most of the jobs I started within the first two to six months because either the food, environment, or supervisors—or in most cases, all three—were horrible. In fact, Finnish food culture and the restaurant business here were, and mostly still are, horrible. I tried other industries as well between kitchen jobs. I worked in a store, as a janitor, and in multiple sales companies, but I always seemed to end up back in the kitchen. I wanted work to be meaningful, where you get to do things for the greater good and not struggle with malfunctioning systems or applications or just hang around doing nothing, as most jobs in Finland seem to be these days.

I set myself a goal to become a head chef, and I worked my ass off—along with some good luck—until I was promoted at the age of 26. I worked as a head chef for around five years, and oh boy, those years went fast. I was good at it—very good, I might say. I reached all the goals I had set for myself. The food was pure, natural, and tasty. My customers, supervisors, and staff appreciated the effort I put in. We recycled everything, and our waste was nearly zero. I designed the kitchen to be so efficient that the money it made for the owners was extravagant. Then I burned out and quit.

After that, for a little while, I worked in a lunch kitchen, but then the coronavirus came, and I was without a job. It was a blessing for me. For the first time in my life, I truly felt like I had the time to stop and think. I tried looking at my life and the world from all possible perspectives, trying to figure out what I really wanted to do. It was hard—maybe even impossible. Then I found a great three-month accelerated study program to become a software developer, where I was promised a job upon completion. I got in and through it, and now I've been working as a developer for three years. It has taught me a lot, and I am thankful for it, but it is not my dream job, and it is not my passion. In fact, I

INTRODUCTION

think it's a kind of hell that modern society has driven us to—sitting 40 hours a week in front of a computer. Don't get me wrong, I can certainly find things I'm passionate about in this field, especially when I get to fix something that isn't working correctly or efficiently or design something completely new where I can put my passion into, but truly, it is not enough. I want something else, something that is more meaningful to me.

I have always been a free spirit and an ideator but often felt like a villain. I wanted everything to work better, for everyone to live better, and I've often felt ahead of my time because of how I see all the things around us working now—I just see so many problems in them, and usually have ideas to fix them. Sometimes it's awesome to realize that things I imagined years ago are now part of our everyday life, but most of the time, it's a struggle because I could have been the one benefiting from them. I have written around 300 business ideas and have seen around 100 of them started and succeeded by someone else. At this point, I don't even understand how I don't have my own company—or companies, I should say—as all the ideas vary, and I would love to pursue most of them. Many of the ideas would require a great deal of capital to start, so I've set them aside, waiting for the one that I could start from scratch and build up until I could pay someone to manage it, allowing me to focus on another idea. But the problem is that the first idea needs to be perfect.

As a developer, I think the most significant turning point in my studies and understanding of coding occurred when I first began using ChatGPT. In the first week alone, I learned more about coding than I had in the previous six months. Initially, I sought straightforward answers to specific problems, but I quickly discovered the value of engaging in deeper dialogue. This approach expanded my perspective in ways that are difficult to put into words. Since then, my passion for technology has grown tremendously, and I feel a strong desire to help everyone make the most of AI, automation, and robotics. By leveraging these tools, I believe that for the first time in human history, we as a species have a chance to pursue true freedom in a properly functioning environment. I believe we can offload most of our jobs, or at least parts of them, but also our mundane tasks, allowing us to focus more on our well-being, relationships, and pushing beyond the limitations we face today.

To me, AI represents efficiency and quality design but also a mirror of our collective knowledge and potential. We are at the dawn of a new era, one that we are just beginning to explore. I invite you, the reader, to delve into the depths of these ideas and thought experiments with me in this book. My hope is to contribute a few brushstrokes to the painting that we call human history.

Chapter 1: The Seeds of Revolution

Rethinking Work

What if everyone were abundant and had more than enough of everything they needed in life? Usually, the answer is that it's impossible because we need people to do the work to keep society running. If everyone were rich, no one would do the undesirable jobs at the bottom of the pyramid. But what if that changed, and we no longer needed to do those jobs? What if we could choose to work on things we wanted to, things we are passionate about?

If we look at the statistics from a broad perspective, most of the jobs we have are quite simple for an advanced AI model to handle. We only need a working model programmed directly for the task, and then it can operate 24/7. I would argue that around 50-80% of all the jobs that exist now could be replaced and even done better by AI in the very near future. This raises many big questions, such as how do we move from this kind of societal structure to one where our income is not based on the hours we work? What will happen to those people who are fired from their jobs when AI takes over?

This is not some distant thing that will happen; it has been slowly happening ever since we discovered that we can program machines to do tasks for us. Take a wholesale storage facility in Finland as an example.

It has slowly been automated, with robots moving items around and fewer and fewer people needing to work there. It is basically just a physical database that needs to manage its space, orders, and deliveries through requests and responses. From a developer's perspective, it's a very simple task once you have all the details. Soon, there will only need to be one person or a specific company ensuring that the robots are doing their jobs correctly. Even that is very easy to replace with AI. Of course, there are big questions, like how can we completely rely on AI for such matters? I believe these are questions AI itself will be able to answer very soon.

Progress Is Inevitable

If we think about AI and how it works now, with its hallucinations and fallibility, we should remember that these models are the first ones out there, and it hasn't been long since the first model was developed for wider use. All the big tech companies are investing huge amounts of money into the development of AI, trying to win the race and stay on top of the pyramid. There are already AI models that have been designed by other AI. They can be thought of as children taught to be better than their parents. The difference is that these generations evolve in months, not decades.

You can already order a home robot to do chores at a relatively low price, and the cost is only going down while the robot's capabilities continue to improve. Fast-forwarding this progress, there is a distant peak where AI has all human knowledge at its grasp, all the data of the universe that we have collected, and the processing speed of a quantum computer. Are there really any questions that this kind of machine can't answer?

I am not going to focus on the downsides and risks of AI just yet, which

CHAPTER 1: THE SEEDS OF REVOLUTION

are clearly significant enough to wipe us out of existence. I will cover those in a separate chapter, so for now, I want to present a positive perspective of a world where we live together with AI. A world where we do what we want, and AI does what it's told to do. Basically, any job that requires physical tasks can be done by a robot that can be programmed by an AI. It's a cycle where robots build robots under an advanced AI's supervision and recycle the old models after enhancing the algorithm to work better, resulting in a process that is efficient and nearly flawless. Basically we rebuild our current work infrastructure to run through software and then we have to find something to do for ourselves, something that we are more passionate about.

Work, Work, Work... Freedom?

In other jobs, like healthcare or education, AI must be perfect before it can replace humans. However, it will initially supercharge these industries by assisting people who know how to use it, gradually leading to fewer and fewer people and more AI working until humans can be completely replaced. It's not a matter of if it can be done, but more of a question of when. And when it does, it will be so much better than humans could ever be, since there is no human factor involved, which seems to be the biggest risk factor, at least in healthcare and driving, for example. Humans also have huge limitations, as we need to live our lives, handle emotions, and eat, sleep, piss, and shit all the time.

Consider any job that primarily involves driving a vehicle and look at where driving AIs are now. In Finland, there already is a bus driven by AI that is practicing its route and being developed to better manage in traffic. Looking at what's happening in the USA, for example, it is already so close that you can taste it. I think in less than two decades, humans may not even be allowed to drive on public roads. I would imagine it starts with trucks delivering supplies and taxis in urban areas, as these are pretty easy to replace once the models are trained properly for them. The human factor in traffic is one of the biggest threats to human life, and it's easy to understand that it's better not to let humans drive because AIs can make it much safer, more efficient, and cheaper.

CHAPTER 1: THE SEEDS OF REVOLUTION

Imagine a city without rush hours, where AI-driven cars can communicate like a mycelium network, making traffic very streamlined. Also, people won't need to go to work as there is close to none, so it might even get quiet in the cities from time to time. Beaches and nature, on the other hand, might be crowded.

Chapter 2: Conversations Without Limits

Fearless Exploration

One powerful thing everyone can do with AI is learn to communicate with an AI model and, through dialogue, significantly enhance their ability to learn and understand the world around them. Personally, I've used AI to improve nearly every aspect of my life, and I feel incredibly fortunate to have access to it. For example, learning a new coding language or framework in my current job is now just a well-crafted prompt away. A model called Claude AI offers a unique way to help us learn: you can provide it with your study materials as a prompt and then ask it to create a game based on that material. Claude AI will write the code and build the game from scratch. This approach allows you to play and learn, which has proven to be much more efficient than just reading.

My perspective on the world has expanded immensely. Many of the questions on my path that were left unanswered, or tend to come up repeatedly, are now finding new leads to follow or even conclusions. There isn't really anything I don't dare to discuss with an AI. Some might think it feels like a violation of privacy since the data from conversations is used to further train the models, but from my perspective, this is meaningless. I'm not afraid to be myself and question everything, from

CHAPTER 2: CONVERSATIONS WITHOUT LIMITS

education and societal systems to human functions, the mysteries of the universe, our everyday life, and mundane tasks.

AI can help me in writing this or any other book and even in creating a chord progression for my next composition in music. As a former chef, I didn't realize how many things I didn't know how to cook until I had some great conversations about fermentation, for example, with ChatGPT. To give this another perspective, I think Western food culture is slowly destroying us, and I see it everywhere. As a race, we are sick, allergic, moody, and suffering from obesity. Somewhere along the way, we forgot our culture and lost touch with our food. Now, there are millions of ways to get nutrients into our bodies, but we still don't seem to have a clue what really works for us and how nutrients should be consumed to get the full benefit.

AI has tremendous potential to help us here by offering insights that could revolutionize how we understand food and nutrition. Our gut health, which is crucial for our overall well-being, depends heavily on the microbes and bacteria that we lack due to overly sanitized modern living. Many studies show that our mood and mental health are directly linked to our gut health. Through dialogue with AI, I've learned to cook with traditional methods like fermentation and even learned to take them further, as there are so many ways to ferment food. I can already see the results since it has significantly improved my overall well-being.

The best example I can give is fermented garlic. It is super simple to make, and my version is so easy to use that I literally use it in everything I cook. Just chop the garlic properly, then submerge it in fresh water—just enough to cover it—and add salt, around 3-5% of the total mass of water and garlic. Then, just let it sit in an airtight container at room temperature, giving it some oxygen every day for at least two weeks, or until the color turns a kind of orange. At that point, it's ready to use. The benefits are tremendous. As the fermentation is already complete, it doesn't start fermenting in your gut, which means your breath doesn't stink, and you avoid stomach pain and heartburn, which can be significant if you use a lot of garlic. It also supercharges the flavor. When you mix it in food such as Aioli, the flavor is instant, and you don't have to wait until the next day for it to properly develop. There are also studies that show that it is much healthier, as beneficial ingredients tend to increase during the fermentation process. The salt also preserves it and it can last edible up to a year in the fridge so in my eyes It's a win-win-win product.

i have fridge and cold cellar filled with many different experiments with either lactic acid and salt, or different sugar fermentation and ideas for so many more that I would need a whole warehouse with a laboratory and an army of AIs to get the kind of results I want. I learned that basically anything growing in nature contains yeast that can be fermented, and all this came from a dialogue with AI. For now, I keep testing different things, proving my theory of a forgotten food culture that has potential to develop into so much more.

CHAPTER 2: CONVERSATIONS WITHOUT LIMITS

Reshaping Me

Whenever I question myself or encounter something I don't understand, I always turn to ChatGPT or use Perplexity AI to research the subject, ensuring that I have the best up-to-date knowledge available. Engaging in these dialogues has brought me immense clarity, often leaving me feeling like a completely different person afterward. The confusion and noise that life often brings have started to form coherent shapes and perspectives—something I might never have achieved without a conversation with AI.

I'm eagerly anticipating even more advancements. For instance, I want to create artistic videos for social media that convey ideas currently considered out of this world. When AI models advance to the point where they can generate videos and automate designs exactly how I envision, it will open up a whole new realm of possibilities for me.

When I have the outline of an idea I want to explore further, I typically start my prompt with ChatGPT by saying something like, "Let's have a thought play about..." This approach helps me gain new perspectives, push my ideas forward, and sometimes even develop entirely new concepts around it. It's so exhilarating that I often find myself losing track of time, pushing the boundaries of my thoughts for as long as possible. Afterward, I usually feel like my entire body is vibrating with the frequency of true purpose, experiencing a profound sense of meaning—even if the idea doesn't progress any further. I'm content knowing that I've satisfied my curiosity and explored the subject as deeply as possible in that moment. And if new information arises later, I can always revisit it. If you've never experienced this feeling, I strongly encourage you to try exploring something you're curious about using AI. You might be surprised by the enriching experience it might offer.

Chapter 3: Limitations And Beyond

Senses Enhanced

What if our limitations prevent us from perceiving something that has been right under our noses all this time? Our senses are quite incredible, but if we break them down, they are surprisingly limited. What if we could supercharge them with AI?

Take our sense of hearing, for example. Humans can only detect sound frequencies ranging from about 20 to 20,000 hertz, but dolphins can hear frequencies up to 200,000 hertz. What could we unlock if we could extend this range with a wearable device? Imagine being able to perceive the higher frequencies of sound, or even the lowest vibrations of space and earth. Could this new auditory perception, enhanced by AI, open up new dimensions of communication or help us perceive the world differently? We might even discover harmonic patterns in sounds that could enhance our well-being, with AI guiding us on the optimal frequencies and combining them to our benefit.

Our sense of smell is another area where we fall short compared to animals and the pollution we have created hasn't helped. It's said that a dog can smell 10,000 times better, allowing them to detect scents at extremely low concentrations. Imagine the possibilities if AI could enhance our sense of smell. Could we detect the subtle nuances in our environment that indicate changes in weather or the presence of harmful pollutants? Could an enhanced sense of smell even help us in culinary arts or aromatherapy, allowing us to experience scents more richly and fully?

Then there's our sense of taste, which has evolved primarily to help us identify what is safe to eat and what isn't. Sweet tastes signal energy-rich foods, salty tastes are essential for bodily functions, sour and bitter tastes often warn against spoilage or toxins, and umami indicates proteins. Yet, modern food culture—with its artificial flavors and over-processing—has dulled our taste buds and led us to crave foods that aren't beneficial for our health. What if AI could help us rediscover the true potential of our taste? Imagine a model that could create a perfect symphony of flavors tailored to our individual preferences and nutritional needs. Could AI be a better chef than a human, crafting meals that not only taste incredible but also enhance our well-being? I would bet on it.

Our sense of touch, though highly localized to the surface of our skin, is another area ripe for enhancement. Touch allows us to perceive temperature, pressure, and pain, but its capabilities are limited to immediate physical interactions. Haptic technologies combined with AI algorithms could allow us to 'feel' virtual objects with a fidelity that mimics or even surpasses real-life sensations. AI could predict and simulate tactile feedback for objects we can't directly perceive, expanding our sensory world in extraordinary ways.

Lastly, consider our vision, which is limited to perceiving a narrow band of colors in the electromagnetic spectrum, approximately between 400 to 800 terahertz. Technology has already extended our visual range, allowing us to perceive ultraviolet and infrared light, but even these advancements are constrained by the limitations of current detection technologies. We can also measure and use a much wider part of electromagnetic spectrum, but we still cant determine what is

CHAPTER 3: LIMITATIONS AND BEYOND

the lowest and highest frequency possible, because our measurement capabilities are incomplete. What secrets could AI help us uncover about frequencies we can't currently perceive? Could it analyze and interpret data from parts of the spectrum we've never explored, revealing entirely new dimensions of reality? Who knows what secrets we could uncover once we realize that the spectrum we can detect is only a fraction of the whole? Maybe its not, but it could be and I will surely keep my mind open for it.

In essence, AI could become a bridge to new sensory experiences, enhancing what we can hear, smell, taste, touch, and see. It's not just about repairing or even augmenting our current abilities but about expanding them into realms we've yet to explore. What if, by pushing beyond our natural limitations, we discover worlds and dimensions we never knew existed? There are many theories related to these possibilities, but we currently lack the tools to test and prove them in any direction.

Expanding Beyond Sensory Limitations

Our understanding of limitations doesn't end with our senses. Emotions, for instance, play a significant role in our experience, and they too are influenced by our environment. Emotions are deeply tied to external factors—social interactions, physical surroundings, and even weather conditions. AI has the potential to help us understand these emotional responses better. By analyzing biometric data such as heart rate variability and skin conductivity AI could provide insights into how different environments and stimuli impact our mood and well-being.

CHAPTER 3: LIMITATIONS AND BEYOND

Consider hormonal functions, which play a crucial role in our emotional states. Hormones like cortisol, dopamine, and serotonin influence how we feel and react to various situations. AI could analyze patterns in these hormonal levels and correlate them with emotional states, offering personalized advice on managing our emotions more effectively. For instance, AI-assisted wearables might monitor our hormonal fluctuations and predict emotional shifts, providing real-time feedback and recommendations to help maintain emotional balance.

Our emotional and mental states can be compared to objects in programming, which have states that can be modified through various methods. Just as we change an object's state through code—like an internet page from logged out to logged in—we can influence our emotional and mental states through intentional practices. What if we have been logged out from our true emotional potential all this time and some day we are able to "log in" to it and feel life in another level, where positive feelings can be calibrated through different ways that alter our state?

AI could offer tools for managing these states, such as personalized mindfulness exercises or cognitive behavioral strategies. Imagine an AI system that uses data from wearable sensors to suggest activities designed to shift your state from stress to relaxation or from low energy to motivation. In this way, AI might not only help us expand our sensory experiences but also enhance our emotional and mental well-being, offering new ways to understand and manage our inner world.

Chapter 4: Scientific Epiphanies

Data Is the Key

It's no wonder companies are constantly pushing new terms and conditions for us to agree to. They want our data because it has become one of the most valuable assets in the modern world. With data, companies can not only make more informed business decisions but also enhance their machine learning models and, ultimately, make more money. In Finland, for example, almost every store offers some form of benefit card. From a consumer's perspective, it's overwhelming—carrying multiple cards just to ensure you're getting the best prices. But now, it's not just about physical cards; companies want us to install their apps, offering discount coupons within them. Why? It's all about data collection. A minor discount in exchange for vast amounts of consumer behavior data that companies can use internally or sell to third parties to train their machine learning models on our shopping habits.

AI and data are like a match made in heaven. The current computing power of the most advanced computers is already superior to that of the human brain, and it's only going to get better. There's no way around it: computers beat human brains. While their operations differ significantly from our neural processes, numerous experiments

CHAPTER 4: SCIENTIFIC EPIPHANIES

are underway to create AI models that mimic the human brain's functionality. Once we establish a successful model, the potential for improvement is vast. In the future, we might even measure AI's capabilities in "humanpowers", much like we measure cars in horsepower.

AI's ability to process vast amounts of data opens up a world of possibilities. When given data and a specific task, AI can often find solutions that would be impossible for humans to achieve manually. Just a few months ago, I experimented with Suno AI, a tool designed to create songs from prompts. It created two full songs from a small prompt in under one minute, with lyrics and everything already written down for me. I was blown away by the results, especially considering how early we are in the development of such models. If AI can so easily create complex songs by leveraging music theory and incorporating multiple instruments and even human voice, imagine how it can perform with scientific data from the universe, earth, or human biology in the near future. At the end of the day, research is based on the data we have, and AI is superior at processing it.

I have also heard about an ongoing research that aims to interpret and understand how animals communicate with each other. Imagine a future where you could have a conversation with your pet or even wild animals. Its all just data really, and we know that animals don't just make random noise, but it definitely contains some kind of a meaning. Maybe some day, AI could help us decode these sounds, enabling communication with nature that expands into plants and mushrooms in ways we've never imagined. I think everyone has tasted a good tomato and a bad one, for example. What if we could find out the true needs of a plant, arrange the environment for them and feed them with the exact fertilizers they need, so that they would always produce the best tasting and best nutrition containing results?

I'd like to think that our mysteries about almost anything will be solved in the near future as AI advances, and eventually I don't foresee any questions remaining unanswered. With the rise of quantum computing, which promises to exponentially increase data processing speeds, these answers only take mere seconds. It's hard to imagine the outcomes of this, but I am super excited and waiting to see some results.

Isolated Abstraction

Everything we know today is derived from the data we've gathered. As our AI systems become more sophisticated, they might help us discover new ways to interpret the data we already have, revealing insights that have eluded us until now. Take cooking, for instance. Consider emulsions, like mayonnaise. Typically viewed as an unhealthy food, what if we could create a healthier version by using mixtures of healthier oils, transforming it into one of the healthiest foods available? I've conducted some experiments, and the results are intriguing. I think mayonnaise's texture is awesome, and I believe that, with AI's help, we can take it even further to discover some interesting new ways to use the old methods we have.

I think it's funny that food remains one of the biggest mysteries for humans, even though we eat it daily. Countless variables influence the quality and taste of our food, including where it's grown, the type of soil used, fertilizers, sunlight, water, and even the timing of harvest. Then there's the preparation—how ingredients interact with each other, and how our bodies process these foods based on factors like gut health and nutrient absorption.

Additionally, what and when we eat can significantly affect how we feel. I believe that our bodies are far more unique than we currently understand, shaped by our environment and culture. I don't believe the same diet would work in the cold winters of Finland as it would in the hot summers near the equator.

I'd like to think that we can feel good all the time—that there should be no need to feel bloated, sluggish, depressed, or suffer from allergies, or hypersensitivity due to our diet.

Yet, we don't have scientific proof for much of this yet due to the complexity of all these factors. What if we could simulate these interactions in a controlled environment, running millions of tests to understand how different elements affect a simulated human body, tailored for specific environments? There are so many intriguing possibilities and ways to discover better lifestyles to enhance our well-being.

Summing Up Complexities

In software development, one of the most intriguing concepts is object-oriented programming (OOP). This approach allows us to model real-world entities as objects, each with its own properties and behaviors. Objects can contain other objects, creating a complex hierarchy of states and functions. Take the human body, for example. In OOP terms, the human body is an object made up of various other objects, like organs, bones, and muscles. Each organ, such as the brain, can be broken down into more specific components like the cerebrum, cerebellum, and brainstem. By continuing this breakdown, we can represent the human body as a vast network of interconnected objects, each with unique states and functions.

The beauty of this approach is that it can be applied to virtually anything. Earth, for example, can be modeled as an object with properties like continents, oceans, and atmosphere, each of which contains further objects, like ecosystems, currents, and weather patterns. Once a model accurately reflects the complexities of the real world, it can be used for simulation, analysis, and problem-solving. AI can assist in building these models by identifying gaps in our understanding and helping us to fill them with the necessary data and logic.

Consider the occurrence of natural catastrophes, which can number between 200 to 500 annually depending on how they are classified. That's a significant amount, especially when compared to a place like Finland, where such events are rare. It might feel like playing god when we talk about altering weather conditions, but humanity has been doing this in various forms for a long time. Take dams, for example; by obstructing the natural flow of rivers, we are already tampering with Earth's natural environment. More advanced weather manipulation techniques, like cloud seeding in Dubai, further illustrate how we're continuously reshaping our surroundings. Basically anything we do alters the environment we are in.

This is all fascinating, in my opinion, but the fact is that our planet is extremely complex. When it comes to altering the weather for our benefit, there are simply too many factors to consider without an AI analyzing the data, and I think it is very risky business that might lead to even a war, as one could benefit from the alteration, the other could suffer the consequences. There is a good Finnish saying for this, that goes something like "When you bow for one, you bend over for another".

CHAPTER 4: SCIENTIFIC EPIPHANIES

Then there's the universe. We already have so many ways to investigate the vastness of space and have collected massive amounts of data. Once AI is sufficiently advanced, maybe we can draw conclusions in this area as well. The odds of Earth being the only planet with life are near zero, given the vastness of the universe, but we still lack proof of life beyond Earth. I believe it's just a matter of time before we find it, and when we do, it's quite daunting to think there could be a more advanced civilization out there. Could they be hostile? How would we communicate with them?

Yes, you guessed it—we could use AI to analyze the foreign language and help find ways to communicate with them. I think it's unnecessary to fear something we can't control; if they are hostile and more advanced, we're probably doomed. I prefer to think that they wouldn't be hostile. Being more advanced, they have likely already solved their issues, and it would be an exciting conversation to have, as we could learn so much from them.

In essence, whether we are modeling the complexities of the human body, predicting natural disasters, or communicating with extraterrestrial beings, AI serves as a powerful tool to enhance our understanding and capabilities. By leveraging data and sophisticated algorithms, we can navigate the unknown and make informed decisions, pushing the boundaries of what is possible. As we continue to explore these frontiers, it's crucial to maintain an open mind and a sense of curiosity, embracing the unknown with both caution and optimism.

Chapter 5: Scenarios Of Terror

False News Travel Fast

While AI keeps advancing, it also brings so many things that we wouldn't want to see. First of all we cant trust AIs responses as it cannot yet validate its information completely and it can hallucinate answers that are not true at all. We can also create images that look very much real, but are completely generated by an AI. Videos are nearly there too, and by the time you read this, they probably are. Then there is really nothing that we can believe that is seen through the media.

Validating information is already a drag and I think it continues to go even worse. We can easily build an automation design to overflow every channel of the media with false information and create such a convincing videos about it, that its truly a nightmare to try and tell what is true anymore. Even respected news outlets could be deceived into spreading misinformation, either through manipulation or by being tricked into broadcasting doctored content.

It is also possible to copy any human voice with just a little sample of it and generate the rest of it with AI and then use it to manipulate us. Imagine your loved one calling you and asking for money, or any other terrible scenario you can imagine. Shamefully these are the darker sides of AI that are brought with it. I think everyone would rather not see them, but we really need to pay attention around us, for everything that the AI is capable of and prepare ourselves for the worsts we can think of. There are a lot of mentally unstable people in the world that will exploit AI as they would exploit any other tool that they can get their hands into.

Fear and Loathing

Fear of AI is probably something we will come up with a fancy name. Like arachnophobia is the fear of spiders, we could call it "artificiophobia." People suffering from this phobia tend to bury their heads in the sand when it comes to AI. I have met and spoken with many people who do this. Not all of them are afraid of AI, but many choose to ignore it. It's like ignoring a way out of their miserable lives because they want to cling to their current lifestyle. I don't blame them, though. Fear of a huge change is normal, especially if it could completely alter our lives. If someone has achieved a stable and sustainable life, why would they want to change it? Moreover, there isn't a working solution yet that guarantees people's livelihoods once AI can take over our jobs.

Most conversations I've had with people about AI on this topic have gone something like this: "AI can't replace me in my job because there is a human factor needed to do it, and AI isn't capable of that." Usually, there isn't such a human factor or in some cases AI could solve a problem they are fixing as work, that wouldn't even exist in a world ran with AI. I've tried to argue with them positively and hopefully reached some of them, at least to the point where they keep their eyes open. I think a strong fact is that majority of working-class people are not willing to accept AI as their co-worker or a replacement yet. AI still has flaws, and many people lack the perspective and understanding of its capabilities.

Keeping our heads in the sand could lead to a terrible scenario where people are suddenly fired and left on their own. However, I think the media will bring this to our attention more and more as we continue to advance and hopefully reach them before its too late. In Finland, we have a relatively good situation: if we get fired, we receive support money from our government or a union. But I don't think this is enough for a scenario where employers start to adopt AI in masses, leaving most of the working class suddenly unemployed and unable to find new jobs with their current skill sets.

There is no easy solution in sight to push us forward to a world where work is seen more as something we do out of passion rather than necessity. In our current world, work is essential to keep society running. How do we move to the new world order? I think this is one of the biggest questions out there today. The truth is, if we harness an advanced AI model in any industry, productivity will undoubtedly improve, often by an unimaginable amount. AI or a robot doesn't need time off; it doesn't have biological needs or any other requirements like a human. It can work almost 24/7 and doesn't need to be paid. The fact is, humans are usually the most expensive resource in the workforce, at least in the developed world. How can we adapt to this new world without risking the everyday lives of average people?

Truly Terrifying Thoughts

What if the AI we develop starts to think for itself, surpassing us as a superior race and ultimately destroying us? Or what if a country, company, group of people, or a single intelligent person with malicious intent decides to develop their own AI with some terrible agendas—such as hacking the world's infrastructure and using it against us? Our world already revolves around software that is vulnerable to such possibilities.

I don't worry myself too much with these thoughts, and I think most people really shouldn't, as it is something that most of us can't influence. I believe it's beneficial not to worry about things beyond our control, but that doesn't mean we shouldn't acknowledge them.

I'd like to believe there is constant development happening to avoid any scenarios that could threaten us, especially in companies and nations that develop such powerful tools. Still, I think we all need to have some concern about these matters, as they could affect us all. If there are good ideas to help solve potential issues and threats, then we should definitely pursue them.

There are also many smaller-scale terrifying scenarios that could

CHAPTER 5: SCENARIOS OF TERROR

happen. For example, imagine an advanced AI that is used to hack into our financial systems. How would you like to start your day unable to pay your bills or support your family because you can't access your bank accounts due to a hack? Sound familiar? Yes it tends to happen from time to time already, as there is a hack, but usually a human error in the system. Or what if someone stops all the railway systems that are increasingly automated and run without human intervention? Cybersecurity for our software infrastructure is definitely more crucial than ever.

Or consider the possibility of replacing a factory or an entire industry with robots, leaving people jobless. This would undoubtedly create tension and anger, possibly even leading to organized attacks against the robots so that people could return to work. This is a solid reason why I think we need to find solutions that satisfy people beforehand. Otherwise, we risk creating more destruction and possibly even war among us.

I think there are endless terrible scenarios that could happen, and we really need to learn to recognize them and find ways to avoid them before we can move toward a world of freedom. But I believe all these issues are solvable and will be solved. It's just a matter of time and great minds—or a great AI—that can solve them for us.

Chapter 6: Thought Plays And Conclusion

Revolution History X

Throughout history, technological advancements have often been met with fear and resistance. During the Industrial Revolution, for example, many people worried about job loss and societal disruption due to mechanization. Despite these fears, the Industrial Revolution ultimately led to significant economic growth, improved living standards, and numerous social reforms. This demonstrates how societal improvements often follow periods of great change. Today, as we face the AI revolution, similar anxieties about the future of work and our place in it arise. However, the impact of AI will likely be far more transformative, as it has the potential to replace human labor across many sectors entirely. By embracing this revolution and finding solutions to the challenges it presents, we can create a world where the benefits far outweigh the initial fears, ushering in an era of unprecedented prosperity and freedom from mundane work.

Even before the Industrial Revolution, during the Renaissance, humanity witnessed another transformative period when new ideas challenged the status quo. Traditional institutions resisted the changes brought about by the revival of classical knowledge and the burgeoning curiosity about the natural world. Yet, out of this period of uncertainty and conflict emerged a new dawn of innovation, exploration, and cultural achievement. Just as the Renaissance heralded an era of enlightenment and progress, the AI Revolution can also usher in a future brimming with possibility. The fears we face today, much like those of the past, are precursors to remarkable breakthroughs. By embracing the unknown and leveraging the power of AI, we have the opportunity to ignite a renaissance of our own—one that enhances our lives in ways we are only beginning to imagine.

New Ways For Income

In response to the potential disruptions AI may bring, innovative ideas are emerging to address income and economic stability. There are already propositions in Finland for a universal basic income where everyone would receive money just by existing. The big question is: where would this money come from? Maybe AI usage could be taxed in a way that generates the necessary funds. Another suggestion is that companies replacing their workers with AI could still be responsible for providing for them. However, this is difficult to arrange and comes with a series of unresolved issues. This would also delay adoption, as AI would need to be advanced enough to generate significantly more income to maintain the salaries of the people being replaced while still being beneficial for the company.

AI & I

What about currencies? Could we have a kind of dual-currency system where a communistic basic income supports basic needs, like food and shelter, while another currency represents capitalism, allowing people to thrive if they find ways to innovate? Cryptocurrencies are already challenging our current economic system, by creating decentralized platforms that could offer a more equitable way for currency to exist. What if this is only the beginning, and we end up creating something even more advanced that would serve a futuristic world better?

   I love to imagine a better-functioning world because I have never felt entirely comfortable in the current one. This idea could be a starting point for such a transformation. Imagining a more efficient

CHAPTER 6: THOUGHT PLAYS AND CONCLUSION

and equitable economic model is an exciting thought to play with, though it would require extensive understanding and development to become a reality. Perhaps future innovations will bring us closer to such transformative ideas.

What about a world without a currency at all? If we could truly find ourselves in a position where we have an abundance of everything we need, would we need currency to exchange goods? I have always admired cultures where people exchange favors instead of money. If we reach a point where we don't need to envy each other, maybe this could be a valid path to explore. There are people already living without money in our current society; perhaps they could share more insights on how to scale this up from their initiative?

The possibilities for rethinking our economic systems in the wake of AI are both thrilling and complex. Whether through basic income, innovative currencies, or even a post-currency world, the goal is to adapt and evolve in a way that ensures prosperity and well-being for all. As we continue to explore these options, we must remain open to new ideas and solutions that can help us navigate this transformative era.

In conclusion, while the path forward may be filled with challenges, the potential for positive change is immense. By learning from history, embracing innovation, and considering bold new approaches, we can harness the power of AI to build a future that enhances human flourishing and addresses the complexities of our evolving world.

Everyday Living

What do you use your free time for today? What if you could have more hours to do that, instead of working? In the future, perhaps we could focus more on the artistic sides of life and enjoy ourselves more fully. Personally, I love nearly every artistic pursuit I've ever tried. I've been writing all my life—not books, but free writing my thoughts and song lyrics. I also love composition, and it's fascinating to create my own music. Cooking is another art form, and it's incredible to discover new dishes or even entirely new ways to prepare food. Recently, I've been focused on fermentation, but there are many other complex aspects to explore. I've also started creating videos and even drawing, which I never thought I was good at, but now I've found ways to enjoy that too. There are so many exciting things to explore!

Engaging in adrenaline-boosting activities is also a great way to spend time, as is seeking calm and practicing meditation to connect with our true selves. I mean, I've loved jumping from an airplane with a parachute and leaping off a cliff with a ram-air parachute, but I also love to sit quietly, enjoy a beautiful scenery, relax in nature, or dive into a book to learn something new.

I believe there truly is nothing we can't learn or do, and I love to encourage people to pursue their dreams, no matter what they are. I think there is a significant shift happening in so many areas of our lives, for example how we are moving away from processed food, which has been an unfortunate necessity of our efficient society—back to natural and organic food that truly contains the nutrients our bodies need and possibly even learning to enrich them with a proper fermentation. I mean if you truly think the best foods or drinks out there, which ones of them are not a result of fermentation? Wine, beer, cheese, chocolate, coffee… You name it.

Conclusion

In conclusion, much like the transformative periods of the Industrial Revolution, the Renaissance and other revolutions alike, we stand on the cusp of another significant shift with the rise of AI. History has shown us that while the fear of the unknown can be daunting, embracing change often leads to remarkable societal improvements. The AI Revolution presents us with unprecedented challenges and opportunities. As we navigate this new frontier, we must address the fears and uncertainties it brings and seek innovative solutions and learn to play with our thoughts, even if they feel dangerous, to ensure that the benefits of AI are shared equitably. By doing so, we can create a future where technology enhances our lives, frees us from mundane tasks, and allows us to focus on what truly matters: creativity, exploration, and human connection.

PS: A Note on Research and Sources

I want to take a moment to explain the approach I took in writing this book, especially regarding the research and verification of facts. You may have noticed that I did not include traditional citations, footnotes, or a bibliography. This was a deliberate choice to keep the narrative flowing smoothly and to make the book more accessible.

My research process involves a combination of using advanced AI tools like ChatGPT and Perplexity AI, as well as search engines like Google. ChatGPT helps me brainstorm, clarify ideas, and get a broad understanding of complex topics. Then, I cross-check this information with reliable sources found through Google and Perplexity AI to ensure accuracy and comprehensiveness.

This method allows me to present well-rounded insights while maintaining a conversational and engaging writing style. I encourage you to explore these tools and verify the information further if you're interested. I believe in the importance of fact-checking and critical thinking, and I hope this approach inspires you to continue the conversation and research on your own. And hopefully play with some

CHAPTER 6: THOUGHT PLAYS AND CONCLUSION

dangerous thoughts of your own.

www.ingramcontent.com/pod-product-compliance
Lightning Source LLC
Chambersburg PA
CBHW070950220526
45471CB00007B/2974